These magical notations belong to:

_____

EVERYDAY MAGIC

A Perpetual Journal
for Spiritual Seekers

CREATED FOR YOU
BY MAIA TOLL

RP STUDIO

PHILADELPHIA

CONTENTS

INTRODUCTION

Each day brings us small bits of magic. Perhaps you research the imagery of a dream and what you learn unlocks a hidden corner of your subconscious. Or maybe you concoct an offhand ritual for heartache and find that it truly heals something that had previously felt broken. Consciously recording serendipities, symbolism, and synchronicities will help train your brain to notice the magic that is perpetually blooming all around you.

But how do you record these daily magics in a meaningful way? Where can you put a note on a recipe, ritual, or bit of research so that you can find the information again when you need it? How can you easily cross-reference between topics (because you might use numerology when looking at astrology and, also, when exploring tarot)?

If you've ever tried to put your magical notations in a chronological journal, you know the frustration of thumbing through the pages wondering, *Did I write the info on the symbolism of feathers in May or was it June? Am I even looking in the right year?*

Exploration of a spiritual and mystical nature requires a different type of notebook—the one you're now holding in your very hands. Welcome to *Everyday Magic: A Perpetual Journal for Spiritual Seekers*, a place to notate your magical life and mystical musings. Most journals are organized by date, making it difficult to revisit your thoughts quickly and easily. *Everyday Magic* is instead organized by topic, so it's easy to retrace your steps and find the exact nugget of knowledge you're searching for. Set up as a perpetual journal, its pages are meant to be filled slowly over time. So, when you learn something new about your stars, for instance, you can add it to the Astrology section; a fresh herbal recipe can be stashed under Plant Medicine; dreams and visions can be recorded in their own section. Because the pages are numbered and organized by subject, you'll be able to cross-reference: if you have a dream in which you wore a red dress, you can record the dream in the Dreams & Journeys section while noting to check out the symbolism of the color red, which you jotted down with information on other colors, under Colors.

This structure makes it easy to flip back to notes, revelations, epiphanies, recipes, and rituals at any point in time. Each page offers space to record however you like best, inviting you to write, draw, doodle, or collage. Additionally, the table of contents can become a study guide, pointing toward areas of learning yet to be explored. *Everyday Magic* is a spiritual scrapbook, waiting to be filled with a lifetime's worth of discoveries.

HOW TO USE THIS JOURNAL

If you're used to starting on the first page of a journal and writing through to the last, then *Everyday Magic* will take some getting used to! To make the most of this journal's format, you're going to have to break some journal writing "rules."

Rules to Break

Start at the first page and write through to the last.

Fill each page before moving on to the next.

Always write in the same direction.

Always use the same color pen or pencil.

Always write.

RECORD BY TOPIC

Instead of simply beginning to write on the first page and continuing through to the last, start by familiarizing yourself with the table of contents. The table of contents is your key to *Everyday Magic* because this notebook is designed to be topical: you are going to record mystical thoughts and events in your life not chronologically but by subject matter.

Don't worry if there are topics in the table of contents that don't interest you at present. *Everyday Magic* is meant to be filled slowly over time. As your interests shift, you'll cycle through various studies; this book holds space for the continuing evolution of your thoughts.

There's a good chance you'll develop some areas of interest not already listed: there are uncategorized pages at the rear of the book so you can add additional topics that speak to your personal magical journey. Be sure to note the topic and the page number in the table of contents so you can easily refer to the notes you record there. If any section that's already noted is too short for your needs, use the blank pages at the end of your journal to continue your explorations.

WHY NOT JUST LOOK UP INFO AS YOU NEED IT?

There are plenty of resources for looking up the symbolism of different colors or the meaning of an animal sighting. Why record your own version?

Each of us understands symbolism and meaning through the filtration system of our own experience. Blue might be the color of your grandma's favorite coat; that very specific recollection, as well as how you felt about your grandmother, will add dimension to any information you research about the symbolism and meaning of blue. *Everyday Magic* is a place to record the specifics of how you perceive the world around you.

HOW DOES THIS WORK IN PRACTICE?

It's surprisingly straightforward! When you have a specific note to make, flip to that section. For instance, if you have a notation on the nature of fire, you'll skip straight to the section titled Elements and jot your note there, even if you still haven't recorded a thing on the first page.

IT'S OKAY TO HAVE BLANK SPACE

Perhaps your note on the nature of fire will be a stand-alone for a bit. Maybe it's just a random thought that crossed your mind while you were lighting a candle one evening: one sentence scribbled on the vast blankness of a page that could, one day, be filled with flames. Having only those few words on an otherwise empty sheet might feel odd to you. It might seem, after writing one thing, that the page is asking to be finished. You *could* try to force yourself to have more thoughts about fire and then intentionally explore the other elements: spirit, air, water, and earth. You *could* . . .

. . . But what if you don't?

What if instead you breathe into the emptiness and let the page remain mostly undisturbed? What if you see the open space as an invitation to your subconscious and, instead of rushing to fill it, wait to see what surfaces? The emptiness, and the invitation to learn more at a later date, is part of the perpetual nature of this journal. Maybe, instead of giving yourself a crash course on the elements, you'll begin exploring the tarot. You'll forget about the fire page and instead start filling pages with thoughts on the symbolism of the major arcana. But eventually, in your tarot studies, you'll want to investigate the symbolism of each suit: cups, pentacles, swords, and wands. You'll realize these suits correspond with the five elements. You'll flip to Elements to begin making some notes there and you'll find your forgotten thought. That lonely notation on the nature of fire will crack open something you weren't quite understanding about the tarot suits. That's how this journal works.

LEAVE BEHIND THE LINEAR

In elementary school, you probably learned how to create a time line: you began at a certain point and worked your way forward by logical, linear steps to arrive somewhere else. Spirituality and magic don't work that way: they simply aren't linear by nature, which is why chronological journaling and record keeping often fail. Mystical thoughts come in webs and spirals, serendipities and synchronicities. And therein lies the magic.

GET CREATIVE!

Use the free-form pages in your *Everyday Magic* journal as an excuse to change things up: write sideways, draw pictures, and glue in photos. Use different colors. Add glitter or stickers. There's no *right* way to do this—only *your* way. Experiment and explore. Not only will this add texture and visual appeal when you later return to a page, it will also invite creativity to be a part of your spiritual and mystical life.

Sometimes your thoughts will defy language. Draw, doodle, collage, or use stamps or scrapbooking supplies—there are many ways to create a record of your thinking!

If you aren't trained in the visual arts, being creative in this way might sound intimidating. The judgmental part of your brain might think things like:

> *"I love looking at other people's creative journals,*
> *but I'm not artistic."*
>
> *"I don't know how to design a creative journal myself."*
>
> *"I don't want to mess up."*
>
> *"I don't know if I can draw well enough."*
>
> *"I'm going to have this journal for a long time,*
> *I want it to be perfect!"*

If your brain is thinking these types of thoughts, assure yourself that *Everyday Magic* is designed especially for you: each page is already laid out and ready to go, no design skills needed! If you feel unsure about your drawing abilities, start simple: color in some of the line drawings in your journal. When you're feeling adventurous, try drawing on a scrap of paper. You can glue it into place later if you like it.

WHY MIGHT YOU WANT TO DRAW?

Perhaps you'll want to remind yourself of the shape of an elderberry's leaves or you might want to record a particularly resonant setup you created on your altar. A simple diagram will suffice for both of these instances. If you doodle a diagram in your journal and don't like what you created, collage on top of it! Allow "mistakes" to create layers and open the door to further creativity.

READY TO BEGIN?

Flip back to the table of contents. Start there and familiarize yourself with the topics included in *Everyday Magic.* If you already know additional topics you want to add, write them into the table of contents and add the appropriate page numbers.

FEELING OVERWHELMED?

Crack your book open to a random page and write a sentence or two about what you know or want to know about the topic you find there. Sometimes you just need to begin. . . it all becomes easier after the first ink mark hits the page.

Remember, some pages or portions of pages may remain blank for a stretch of time. That emptiness is part of the magic: it's the space you're holding for new information and insight. Your *Everyday Magic* journal will evolve as *you* evolve, unfolding in its own mysterious (and magical!) way.

INTENTIONS

Setting a clear, specific intention is like drawing a map for your psyche. It's an opportunity for you to tell yourself where you want your life to go. When you are setting an intention, dig deep and figure out what you want on the most fundamental level. For example, if you're searching for a partner, it's easy to think about the externals: what they look like or what kind of music they listen to. Dig deeper. What do you want to feel when you find your partner? What sort of life do you intend to have together? Maybe, what you're most looking for is to feel loved, cherished, and seen for who you really are. That, then, becomes your intention.

Oftentimes intention setting works best when you can be specific about the emotions you want to feel while leaving some wiggle room for how, exactly, these goals will be achieved!

Note your intentions and the date you set them. Sometimes it takes a while but it's truly amazing how your intentions will manifest when given time. Tracking them allows you greater insight into this process.

CYCLES

Cycles show us repeating patterns. Once you know the pattern, you can work with the energy it generates.

BREATH

The first cycle is breath. When you are born, the first thing you do is inhale. When you die, your last act is an exhale. In many mystical traditions, the soul is inhaled on your first breath and exhaled on your last.

Breath is the most intimate cycle—the sharing of breath is our first communion. For this reason, breathing exercises are central to spiritual studies. Use these pages to note exercises you experiment with. Remember to note down not only how to do the exercise but also how it made you feel.

DAY & NIGHT

Day and night are the yang and yin of every 24-hour cycle. It's said that the in-between times—dusk and dawn—are interstitial moments that open us up to magic, to change. In traditional Chinese medicine, each organ has a specific time in the 24-hour cycle when it does its detoxing and healing. Are there certain times that work best for you for various rituals? Have you learned of times when healing herbs should be harvested?

Use these pages to make notes about time and how you use it in your spiritual practice.

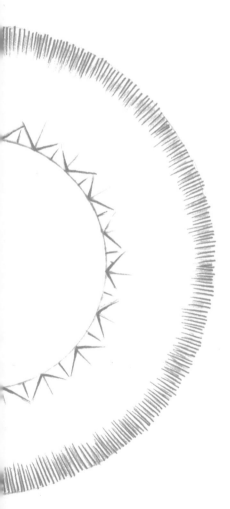

24

THE PHASES OF THE MOON

Every month, the moon moves from new to full and back again. This cycle of expansion and contraction influences the energy of our own month: grow projects and ideas as the moon expands and release stale energies as the moon contracts. Use New Moon energy to incubate fresh ideas and Full Moon energy to celebrate completion.

These pages are the place to record your observations on the moon's cycle, including how *you* cycle with the moon. Take note of your own patterns and how you respond to lunar shifts.

New Moon

Quarter Moon

Half Moon

Three-Quarter Moon

Full Moon

THE CIRCLE OF THE YEAR

The seasons teach us about yearly changes that happen in the natural world and metaphorically throughout the phases of our own lives. The cycle begins in winter when the earth is frozen. This is an inner time, a womb time, a waiting time. As the world thaws, new life emerges growing through the spring to come into full flower in the summer. Flowering is a creative act, a full outward expression. As summer shifts to autumn, energy begins to sink in preparation for winter, for the going inward. What's not needed is let go and roots are strengthened. This is harvest time when we ask ourselves, What have I grown and nurtured this year?

Use these pages to note your thoughts on the seasonal cycles as well as seasonal celebrations and rituals.

SYSTEMS

ASTROLOGY

For thousands of years, astrology has been practiced across a wide range of cultures. People looked to the stars to know when to plant crops and when to harvest. The positions of the celestial bodies predicted the changing of the seasons before they were used to predict the seasons of an individual person's life.

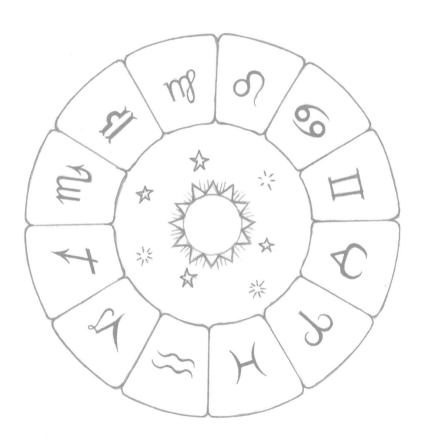

The Wheel of the Stars

Our solar system rotates through a sea of stars. The constellations that align to form a backdrop against which we cycle through are called the zodiac. The sun moves through a new sign of the zodiac every month, the moon does so every two to three days, and the planets visit at various speeds relative to their own laws of motion.

After the Renaissance, the zodiac signs were grouped in two ways:

1) They were each assigned an elemental correspondence: spirit, earth, air, water, fire. See Symbols & Correspondences: Elements on page 119.

2) They were divided into "qualities": cardinal, fixed, and mutable.

   CARDINAL: *start a new season, therefore focused on beginnings.*

   FIXED: *occur at the height of the seasonal energy and represent the season's fullest expression.*

   MUTABLE: *End each season. They are transitioning to what's next.*

The Twelve Signs of the Zodiac

Aries

FIRE, CARDINAL

Taurus

EARTH, FIXED

Gemini

AIR, MUTABLE

Cancer

WATER, CARDINAL

Leo
FIRE, FIXED

Virgo
EARTH, MUTABLE

Libra

AIR, CARDINAL

Scorpio

WATER, FIXED

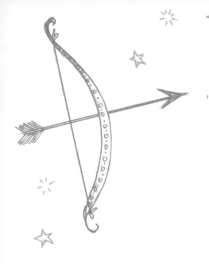

Sagittarius

FIRE, MUTABLE

Capricorn

EARTH, CARDINAL

Aquarius

AIR, FIXED

Pisces

WATER, MUTABLE

The Moon & The Stars

The moon moves through a new zodiac sign every two to three days. To notice the effect this has on you, track your moods and emotions through a few cycles.

Moon in Aries

Moon in Taurus

Moon in Gemini

Moon in Cancer

Moon in Leo

Moon in Virgo

Moon in Libra

Moon in Scorpio

Moon in Sagittarius

Moon in Capricorn

Moon in Aquarius

Moon in Pisces

The Celestial Bodies

Each celestial body has its own energy. Use this space to make notes as you learn about them.

Sun

Moon

Mercury

Venus

Mars

Jupiter

68

Saturn

Uranus

Neptune

Pluto

Your Planets & the Stars

Use this chart to map where the stars and planets were when you were born. You can look up this information online.

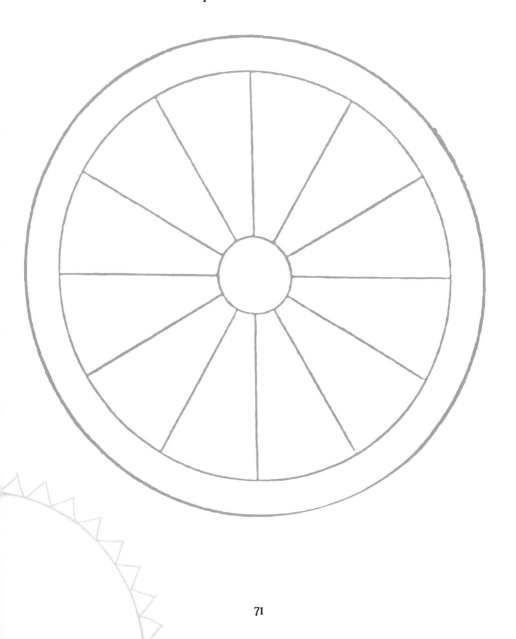

1st House

2nd House

3rd House

4th House

5th House

6th House

7th House

8th House

9th House

10th House

11th House

12th House

TAROT

Tarot began as a game in the northern Italian city-states. It's first mentioned in the mid-1400s but, because of the complexity of the game at that point, it's suspected to have an earlier origination. It wasn't until the nineteenth century that it became associated with divination.

THE MAJOR ARCANA *represent archetypes: universal examples of behaviors, concepts, or personalities. These cards show us the larger patterns of our own behaviors or the paths our lives might take.*

THE COURT CARDS *reflect oneself and the people one might encounter in one's daily life. In the original decks, these cards reflected the titles of people in the royal court. Decks have diversified in modern times, so note that the titles on your particular deck might need to be matched to these original names.*

THE MINOR ARCANA *are divided into suits. Each card can best be understood as a combination of the energy of the suit married to the energetics of the card's number (see Numbers, page 115).*

Use the pages that follow to make your notes as you learn tarot.

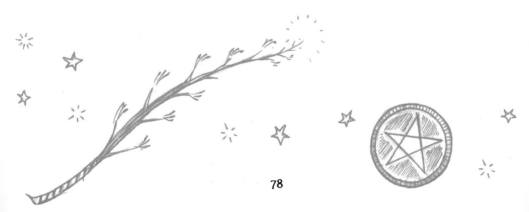

79

0, The Fool

MAJOR ARCANA

I, The Magician

III, The Empress

MAJOR ARCANA

IV, The Emperor

MAJOR ARCANA

V, The Hierophant

VI, The Lovers

VII, The Chariot

VIII, Justice

MAJOR ARCANA

IX, The Hermit

X, Wheel of Fortune

XI, Strength

MAJOR ARCANA

XIII, Death

XIV, Temperance

XV, The Devil

XVI, The Tower

MAJOR ARCANA

XVII, The Star

XVIII, The Moon

XIX, The Sun

MAJOR ARCANA

XX, Judgment

XXI, The World

MAJOR ARCANA

Page

COURT CARDS

Knight

Queen

King

Wands

SUITS

Cups

SUITS

Pentacles

SUITS

THE CHAKRA SYSTEM

During both the Victorian era and the New Age movement, Western spiritualists became fascinated with Eastern philosophies. They used the Hindu *cakra* system to form the basis for the concept of the chakras used today. *Cakra* which means wheel, disk, and circular is also a word used to refer to the sun. *Cakras* are our inner suns: centers of vitality within the physical human body. This has been adapted into the chakra system in which each energy center is associated with our psychic body. While this particular system is Hindu in origin, many of the world's cultures acknowledge a system of energetic bodies with correspondences to the physical body.

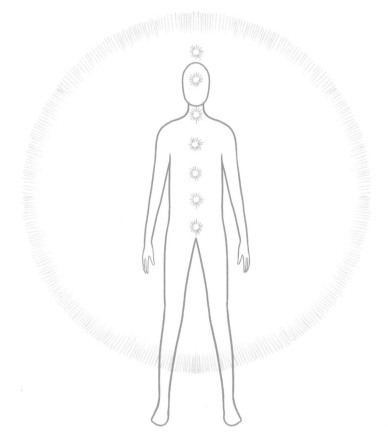

Root

Sacral

Solar Plexus

Heart

Throat

Third Eye

Crown

Hands

Additional Chakras

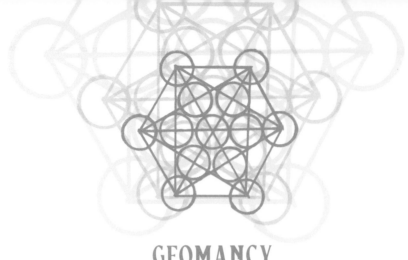

GEOMANCY

(LEY LINES, FENG SHUI, VASTU SHASTRA, ETC)

How do you lay out a space for best energy flow? How is the Earth laid out for energy flow? Put your notes here!

ADDITIONAL DIVINATION SYSTEMS
(RUNES, OGHAM, MUDRAS, ETC.)

There are a myriad of divination systems you might choose to study. Use this place to record your learnings.

HEALING SYSTEMS

(TRADITIONAL CHINESE MEDICINE, AYURVEDA, REIKI, ETC.)

Every culture has its own system for health and wellness. Most pre-modern systems have mystical aspects. Use this space to record your learnings.

SYMBOLS & CORRESPONDENCES

Symbols and their correspondences help us find our way in a mystical landscape. In this section, there's space to explore the symbolism of numbers, colors, the elements, archetypes, personal guides, and power items.

NUMBERS

The earliest philosophers believed that the universe could be explained through mathematics. *Gematria*, the practice of assigning numerical values to words, dates back thousands of years. The modern practice of this is called numerology.

COLORS

Colors come up in dreams and visions as well as in interpretations of symbolism. While these meanings are used in mysticism, they are also important in psychology and art history.

ELEMENTS

The elements are used in everything from healing to astrology to tarot. Use this space to record your thoughts on the traditional four elements as well as the fifth element, which is sometimes called "ether" or "spirit."

Spirit

Air

Earth

Water

Fire

ANIMALS

Because of our shared consciousness, animals have long captured our imagination. They have been an important part of human iconography for thousands of years and their visitations resonate on both a conscious and subconscious level. Record your learnings on their symbolism, as well as meaningful visitations, here.

ARCHETYPAL SYMBOLISM

What symbols appear over and over in your life and what do they mean? Common symbols include a doorway, a circle, a spiral, a seed, a key, a crossroads, and a mirror. Notice your symbols and use this space to make notes on their meanings.

PERSONAL GUIDES, GUARDIANS, AND FAMILIARS

Sometimes you connect with an animal in a unique way; a character from a show or book; the spirit of an ancestor; or an element of the landscape. They become alive and present for you. For instance, you might start seeing owls all the time or hear your great uncle's voice in your head when you are working through a problem.

Who are the spirit messengers and teachers in your life? Who or what appears in your dreams and on your journeys to guide you on your way? What archetypes or characters pop into your mind when you're trying to solve a problem? These pages are to note what they share and how you honor them.

PERSONAL POWER ITEMS

What objects feel imbued with personal power? Maybe it's your great grandma's wedding band or a stone you found on a hike. In the moment, it may seem that you'll carry a particular object with you forever, but the truth is, over time, we swap out these items. It's useful to have an inventory of objects that have meaning for you so you can return to them again when you need to re-energize a particular part of your life. Be sure to note the object as well as its meaning or symbolism (this might change over time, so note that too!).

RITUALS

Rituals can be used for a myriad of reasons including:

Cleansing & Clearing

Attracting & Calling In

Creating Sacred Space

Communing with Animals & Ancestors

Seasonal Celebrations

Gratitude, Love, and Happiness

Grounding

Protection

Building an Altar

A ritual can take a breath or many days. It can be personal or public. Take note of rituals you use and their purpose. Recording specific ingredients or tools as well as time of day, time of year, and phases of the moon can help you recreate a successful ritual.

DREAMS & JOURNEYS

Sometimes it takes days or even months for the whisperings of your subconscious to make sense in your waking life. And yet, we often know when we've had a meaningful dream or vision—one that we will want to revisit over and over. Record those deeply resonant dreams, journeys, and visions here. Try to include not just the substance of your dream but also when it occurred, including time of year, moon phase, etc.

SERENDIPITIES & SYNCHRONICITIES

You find a feather moments after you make a big decision. You get exactly the message you need from a fortune cookie. These are the small, secret messages you're constantly receiving—if you are open to them.

Keep track of the whisperings from the universe here.

GRATITUDES

Keeping track of what you're grateful for reminds you of what you love. Return to this page when you need a little personal medicine. It's like writing a love note to your own life.

HEALING TOOLS

How do you heal on both a physical and spiritual level? Note what has worked for you so you're able to return to the tools that most resonate.

This is also the how-to section of your notebook! What did you put in your protection incense? What tea helped your heart when a loved one died?

When you create a ritual for healing, a recipe for wellness, or create a sacred object, put the details here.

ENERGY MEDICINE &
HEALING RITUALS

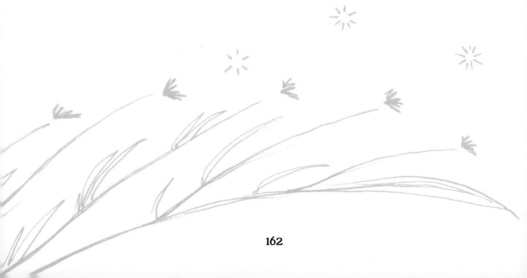

CRYSTALS

PLANT MEDICINE
(HERBS, OILS, FLOWER ESSENCES)

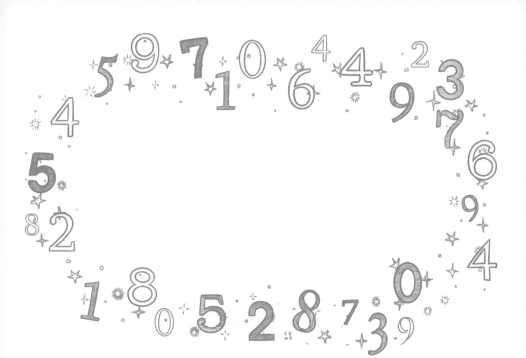

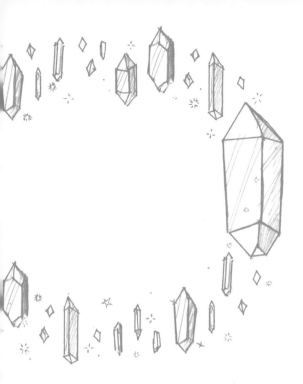

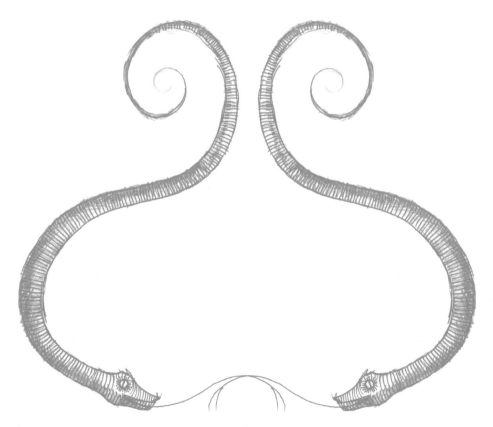

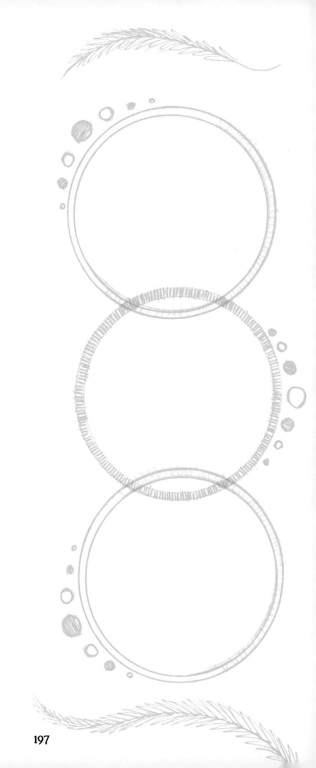

RP Studio™
Hachette Book Group
1290 Avenue of the Americas, New York, NY 10104
www.runningpress.com
@Running_Press

Printed in Malaysia

First Edition: September 2023

Published by RP Studio, an imprint of Perseus Books, LLC,
a subsidiary of Hachette Book Group, Inc. The RP Studio name and logo
are trademarks of the Hachette Book Group.

Running Press books may be purchased in bulk for business, educational, or
promotional use. For more information, please contact your local bookseller or the
Hachette Book Group Special Markets Department at Special.Markets@hbgusa.com.

The publisher is not responsible for websites (or their content)
that are not owned by the publisher.

Design by Susan Van Horn.

ISBN: 978-0-7624-8283-2

APS

10 9 8 7 6 5 4 3 2 1

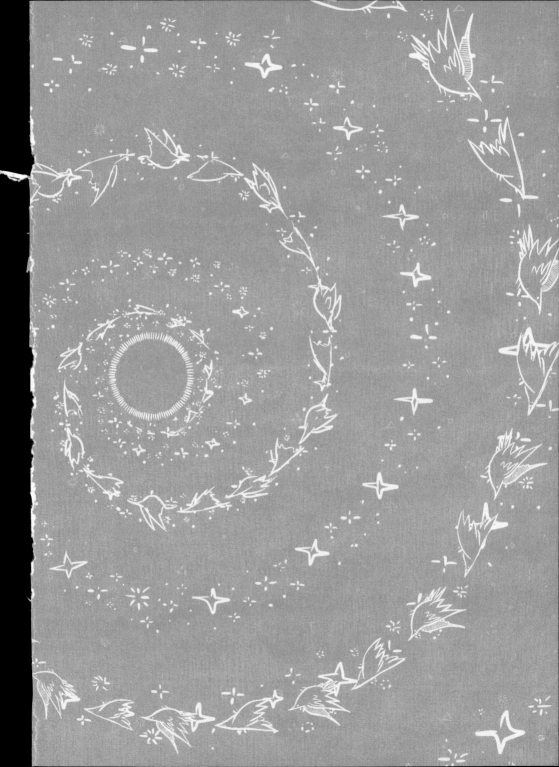